First Facts®

Earn It, Save It, Spend It!

T0052304

Save Money

by Mary Reina

PEBBLE
a capstone imprint

First Facts are published by Pebble
1710 Roe Crest Drive, North Mankato, Minnesota 56003
www.mycapstone.com

Library of Congress Cataloging-in-Publication Data
Names: Reina, Mary, author.
Title: Save money / by Mary Reina.
Description: North Mankato, Minnesota : Pebble, [2020] | Series: First facts.
  Earn it, save it, spend it! | Includes index.
Identifiers: LCCN 2018060537| ISBN 9781977108326 (hardcover) |
  ISBN 9781977110039 (pbk.) | ISBN 9781977108524 (ebook pdf)
Subjects: LCSH: Money—Juvenile literature. | Savings accounts—Juvenile
  literature.
Classification: LCC HG221.5 .R453 2019 | DDC 332.024—dc23
LC record available at https://lccn.loc.gov/2018060537

Editorial Credits
Karen Aleo, editor; Sarah Bennett, designer; Tracy Cummins, media researcher;
Kathy McColley, production specialist

Photo Credits
Alamy: Tetra Images, LLC, 19; Capstone Studio: Karon Dubke, Design Element,
Back Cover, 17; iStockphoto: Alina555, 13, ivanastar, 7 Right, SelectStock, 11;
Shutterstock: anythings, 21, Doubletree Studio, 15, Forgem, Design Element,
Monkey Business Images, 5, monticello, 7 Left, Nik Merkulov, Design Element,
Sergey Ryzhov, 9, Thomas J. Sebourn, Cover

All internet sites appearing in back matter were available and accurate when this book was sent to press.

Printed and bound in China.
1671

Table of Contents

CHAPTER 1

It's Great to Save

Everybody needs money. One of the best ways to have money is to **save** it. You put it aside and add more when you can. Saving money lets you buy the things you need and the things you want.

Fact

Saving money can help you with things you don't expect but may come up later. What will happen if a strap on your backpack breaks? You will have the money to fix it.

save—to put money away so you have it in the future

What is the difference between a need and want? Needs are things you must have. Food, clothes, and school supplies are needs. You like wants, but can do without them. Video games, toys, and tickets to a movie are wants.

Needs

Wants

You may not save enough money to buy all your needs and wants. Then you will have to make a choice. Your needs should come first. You can still buy some of your wants. All you have to do is keep saving.

Needs and Wants

How do you choose between needs and wants? Let's look at an example. You need markers for school. You want the watercolor markers because a friend has them. Needs are more important than wants. You might buy a regular set of markers to save money.

Saving Choices

It's easy to save at home with a glass jar. Fill the jar with money you **earn**. Some young people earn money by helping at home. Others get an **allowance**. Some get money as a gift for birthdays and holidays. You can add the money you get to the jar.

earn—to receive payment for working

allowance—money given to someone at a set time

A **savings account** at a bank is another way to save. An adult can help you open it. Banks are places that hold money and keep it safe. You fill out a slip to **deposit** money in the account. You fill out another slip to **withdraw** money. You can check your account online too.

FACT

Banks offer different types of accounts. One type of account helps pay for a college education. Banks have ways to help make the money grow.

savings account—an account at the bank in which you store money

deposit—to put money into a bank account

withdraw—to take money out of a bank account

Many people **invest** money. They use their money to make more money. As an example, banks offer free money with a savings account. It is called **interest**. The bank adds the money to a person's savings over time.

FACT

Banks lend money to people who need it. This is called a **loan**. Banks charge interest for the loan. People pay back more than they receive.

invest—to give or lend money now so you can earn more money on it

interest—the cost of borrowing money

loan—money that is borrowed with a plan to pay it back

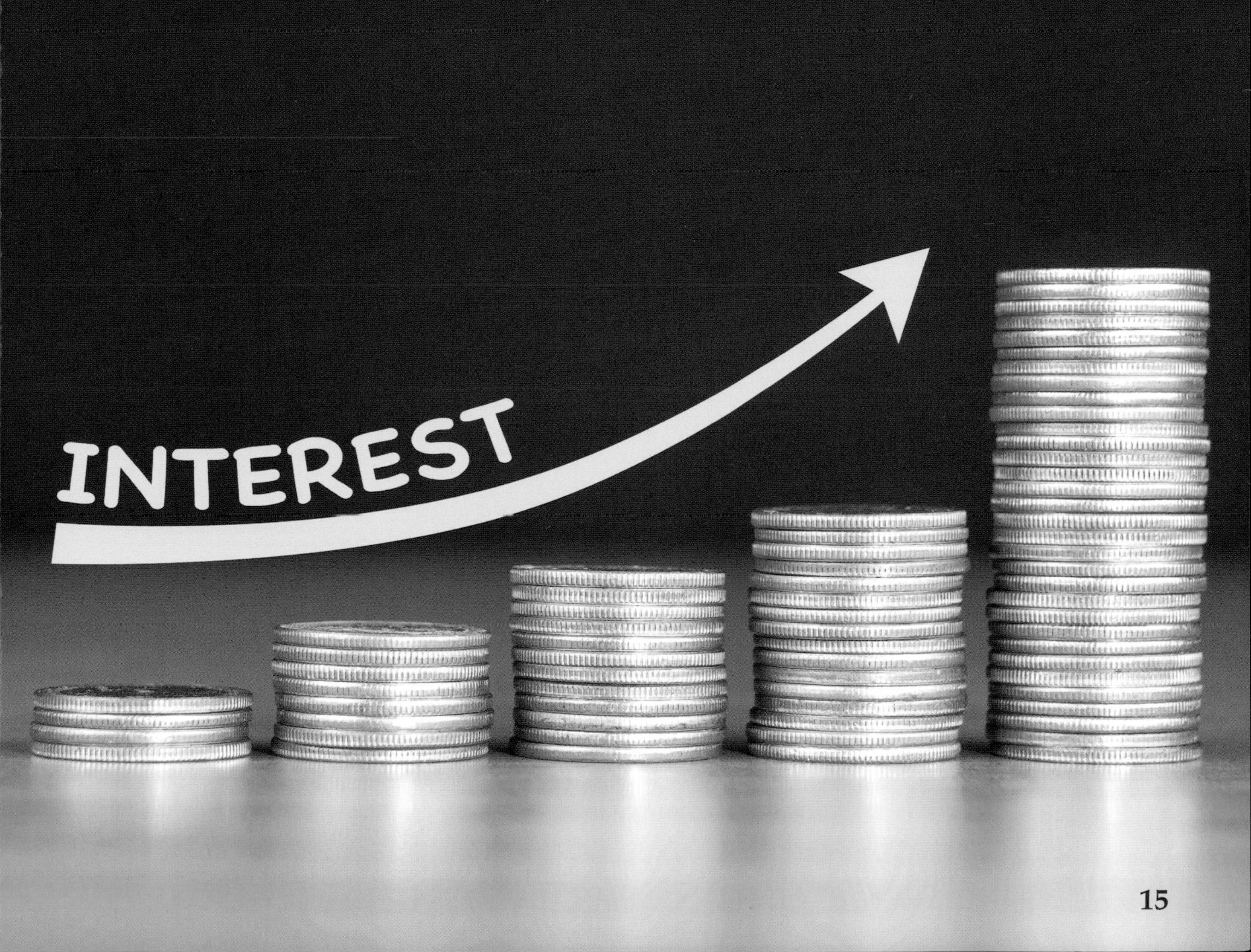
INTEREST

Try It!

Here is a fun way to help you
keep track of your savings. An adult
can help you set up this project. It
will show how money goes into and
comes out of a savings account. It will
also help you save for the future. All
you need is a jar and a notebook.

Set up a page in the notebook like the Savings Chart. Fill in the chart each time you save money. Do the same when you take money out. Count the money that is left. Write the amount on the chart.

Keep Saving

When the jar fills up, you can put the money in a savings account. Then start filling the jar again. You can add it to the savings account, buy something special, or **donate** it. When you donate money, you give it to a person in need.

donate—to give something as a gift to a charity or cause

Savings Chart

Date	Deposit	Withdraw	Total Money Saved
December 1	$1.00		$1.00
December 15		$0.50	$0.50
January 10	$2.00		$2.50

Try to fill the jar by a certain date. You could pick your next birthday. You might pick a favorite holiday. Saving enough to fill the jar will depend on the choices you make.

You will always have needs and wants. Saving money will make getting them easier and a lot more fun.

Glossary

allowance (ah-LAU-uhns)—money given to someone at a set time

deposit (di-PAH-zuht)—to put money into a bank account

donate (DOH-nayt)—to give something as a gift to a charity or cause

earn (UHRN)—to receive payment for working

interest (IN-trist)—the cost of borrowing money

invest (in-VEST)—to give or lend money now so you can have more money on it

loan (LOHN)—money that is borrowed with a plan to pay it back

save (SAYV)—to put money away so you have it in the future

savings account (SAYV-ings uh-KOUNT)—an account at the bank in which you store money

withdraw (with-DRAW)—to take money out of a bank account

Read More

Bullard, Lisa. *Lily Learns about Wants and Needs*. Money Basics. Minncapolis: Millbrook Books, 2014.

Higgins, Nadia. *Saving Money*. Money Smarts. Minncapolis: Jump!, 2018.

Reina, Mary. *Save Money*. Money and You. North Mankato, MN: Capstone, 2015.

Internet Sites

The Mint: It Makes Perfect Cents
http://www.themint.org/kids/

Sesame Street: Finances for Kids
https://www.sesamestreet.org/toolkits/save

Critical Thinking Questions

1. Pretend you are thinking about buying a new backpack for school. The one you have is still good. Is it a need or a want?

2. How can you invest money?

3. What are reasons for saving?

Index